Caricature Relief Carving
with Larry Green

Pattern design by Mike Altman
Photography by Steve Smith
Creative Consultant, Lee Warren

77 Lower Valley Road, Atglen, PA 19310

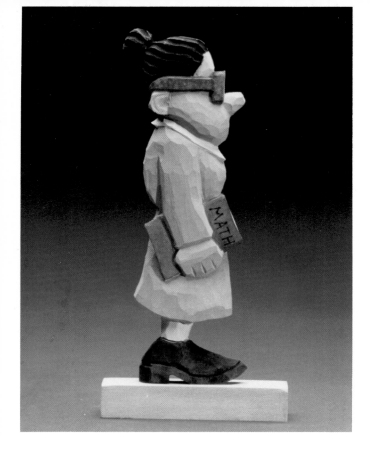

Designed by Bonnie Hensley

Copyright © 1993 by Larry Green.
Library of Congress Catalog Number: 93-84624.

Printed in the United States of America.
ISBN: 0-88740-542-8

Published by Schiffer Publishing, Ltd.
77 Lower Valley Road
Atglen, PA 19310
Please write for a free catalog.
This book may be purchased from the publisher.
Please include $2.95 postage.
Try your bookstore first.

We are interested in hearing from authors
with book ideas on related subjects.

DEDICATION

From Larry:
    To my wife Myra and son Jeff who encourage me to keep carving.
    To Lee Warren, Master Woodcarver at the Dollywood Entertainment Park, thanks for your insight, instruction and inspiration.

From Mike:
    Mom and Dad - without whom Larry would've had to find another artist.
    Miss Pea - without you...we'd have done the book anyways...it just wouldn't have been as "interesting".

Contents

Introduction

Mike and I were working on a carving project when I asked him to create a pattern for a Tennessee Mountain Man. I can't draw, and Mike is a really poor wood carver. (Just look at the Band-Aids on his fingers.) From that one drawing, we combined our talents and started brainstorming with Mike drawing and me carving. The result is a host of creative caricatures which we think will give you hours of carving enjoyment and bring smiles to the faces of people who see them.

You will quickly see we have kept some of the patterns fairly simple. For example, the fireman has no eyes, ears, or hands to carve. You will also see

that none of the patterns except the bride, groom and the wood worker, have mouths. The bride and groom just needed to have smiles. We put a mouth on the wood worker so we could place small nails in the corner of it. Should you choose, you can add a mouth to any of the carvings with a v-tool or your knife. We have included some difficult designs which we hope will provide you with a challenge.

The wood worker is my favorite... no maybe the scuba driver... no the ice skater. It was difficult to decide which patterns to include in the book. We currently have over 150 designs in our portfolio. They range from the very simple to the complex. The piano player and computer lady in the book are what Mike and I call an *American Scene*: a caricature and defining object which portrays life in America.

I chose the thin ¾" wood to achieve the excitement of carving the caricatures in relief. My goal is to give the figure a rounded look and trick the observer's eyes into thinking the carving is round rather than flat. One key to this effect is determining how deep to cut certain features (such as a hand, arm, or tool) and how much or what type of angle to give to other features. The carvings look their best when painted. Through highlighting and shading with paint, you will be able to add even more illusion of depth. As always, practice in using paints will be the key to making your figure appear more three dimensional. Viewing the carving from a few feet away will tell you if you have succeeded.

The flat style of carving presented in this book lends itself to several uses. You can mount the completed caricature on a base. You may want to hang one on the wall. Or you may want to mount the carving to a board and make a plaque. The Gallery in the back illustrates some of the uses of the carvings.

If you're not into relief carving, we hope you will consider our designs for "in the round" carving.

Getting Started

The following tools are beneficial in carving the caricatures. Of course, the more variety in your tools the more flexibility to texture the surface.

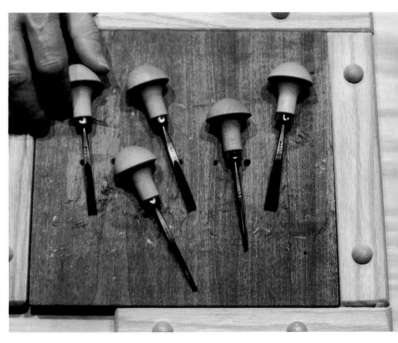

A set of palm gouges.

A knife: The knives in the book are made by Ken Helvie of Indiana. These are excellent quality custom knives made with tungsten carbon steel and Packawood handles. Packawood is made of selected hardwood veneer which has been vacuum impregnated with color dyes and phenolic resins. The veneer is bonded together under pressure and high temperature to form a multi-layer wood laminate.

A variety of larger gouges including a 5/16" 60 degree V-tool, a 10mm 90 degree V-tool, a 5/8" No. 2 sweep gouge, a 3/4" No. 3 sweep gouge, and a 3/16" veiner and not pictured (1/2" chisel and 6mm 90 degree v-tool) are all very helpful.

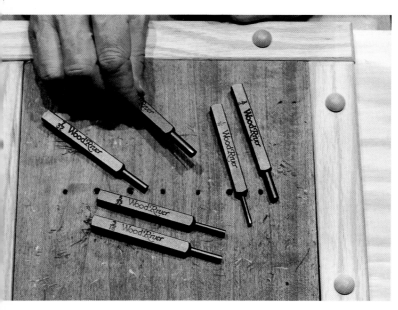

Some carver's eye punches. These are helpful aids for making buttons and designs.

I prefer to do the majority of the caricature carving on a simple carving board which holds the project. To finish the carving, however, you will need to hold the project in your hand. As you practice and understand what caricature relief carving involves, you might discover a better method for yourself. My board is a ¾" x 9" x 9" yellow poplar board with a Walnut Minwax stain. I found the center line of the board and drilled 7 holes 3/16" in diameter, 1" apart the length of the board with the grain running perpendicular to the line of holes.

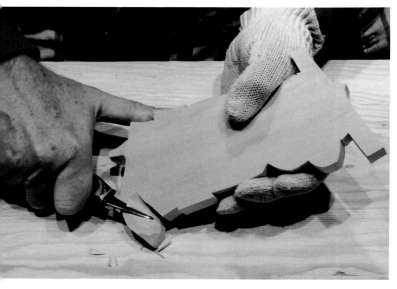

To carve the caricatures, you can use one of two production methods. You can do all the carving by holding the project in your hand. I have a friend who prefers to carve the caricatures in this manner. If you elect to use only this method, I suggest a woodcarver's safety glove. It's a helpful item just in case the knife or gouge takes on a mind of its own.

I counter sink the holes on the back side of the board. I use two #10 x 1¼" flathead wood screws to hold the project. Don't use screws that are too long or you might cut into one, dulling your chisel and ruining the carving.

The board needs to be secured to your work bench. You can use C-clamps.

Or you can secure the board in a vise.

I made the **LARC Frame's** base 24" long so I could use two C-clamps to secure the frame to my work bench. The 24" base allows room to get the C-clamps out of the way. Of course, you could screw the frame base to your work bench. You might even want to try a Black and Decker Workmate. This picture shows the carving board surrounded by the **LARC Frame**. The carving board simply lays inside the frame. It should fit snug in the frame yet be loose enough so you can lift it out and rotate it to the desired position.

As you carve the caricatures, you will discover you need to rotate the board from time to time to obtain the best carving angle. If you use the C-clamps to secure your board, you will have to undo and then redo the clamps each time you want to rotate the board. Using the vise is better, but you still have to fiddle with it when you want to rotate the carving board.

I chose to build a frame for the board rather than use the C-clamps or vise to hold the carving board. I call it the **LARC FRAME** (**La**rry's **R**elief **C**arving Frame). Using the **LARC FRAME**, will allow you to rotate the carving board without any fuss or trouble. I built the frame using wood screws to attach ¾" thick by 1½" wide strips of wood to a ¾" x 12" x 24" plywood board. I left a 2½" space so I could easily remove wood chips which fall off the carving board into the frame when I rotate it. You don't have to build the **LARC FRAME** to carve the caricatures. You don't need the carving board either, but I have found both to be very helpful.

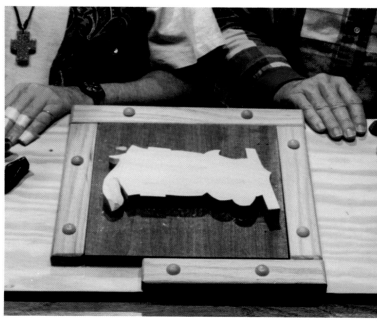

CARVING THE CARICATURES

1. Don't become so focused on carving that you forget about your hand placement. Keep your free hand out of the path of the gouge.

2. I have found that its best to first cut back the area that needs to be cut back the deepest. In most cases, those cuts are going to be in the leg and shoe area.

3. At times, I have found it helpful to use a small carvers mallet with my gouges.

4. If you choose to use the carving board and **LARC FRAME**, when you remove the project from the carving board, you will need to cut away the saw marks and then finish any details which needs to be done on the ¾" edge. For example, the wrinkles on the cowboy's bandana will have to be finished with your knife or v-tool when the carving has been removed from the carving board.

5. Because of the thickness of the wood, I believe it is helpful to create a base for the carvings. Although, not necessary, it will help the carving stand better and prevent the toe on a long shoe from breaking.

6. I choose not to add a lot of detail to most of the carvings pictured in the Gallery. Our patterns, however, do invite more details. Adding details will make the carvings more yours.

FINISHING YOUR CARVINGS

To detail the projects, I paint the figures with acrylic paints such as Ceramcoat by Delta. If I want the carving to have a bright look, I use the paint straight from the bottle. On most of the carvings, I prefer to dilute the paint with water to create a wash. You can create your wash with any ratio of paint to water. For example, a light wash might be 30% paint and 70% water. If you're not sure of what your wash will produce, you can always experiment on a piece of scrap wood. Because of the thickness of the wood, highlighting and shading with paint is important. With a little practice, you will learn where to add some highlighting and shading to bring out details. Antiquing your carving will also aid in bringing out detail. Antiquing will fill in the cuts and grooves and thus give the illusion of more depth. There are many brands of antiquing medium on the market. Choose one which works well for you. Don't be afraid to experiment.

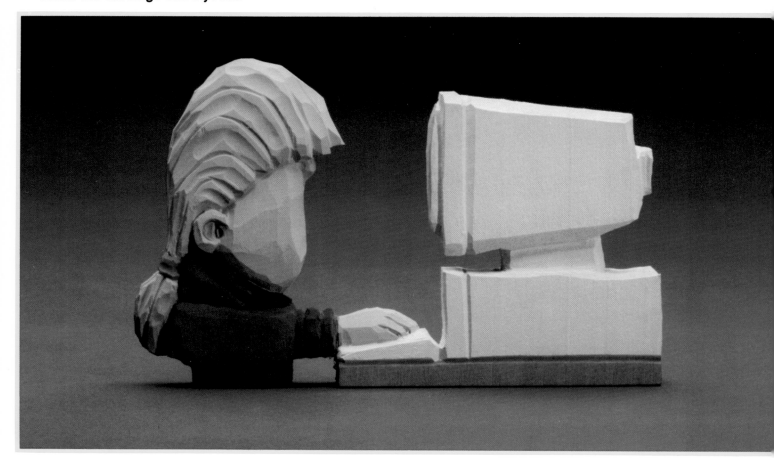

Graduate

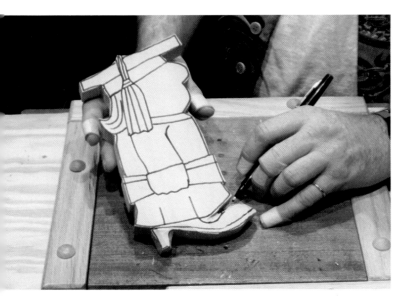

Use carbon paper to transfer the pattern to a ¾" thick piece of wood. The grain runs head to toe. Cut your pattern out with a band saw, coping, or scroll saw.

If you choose to use the carving board approach, then attach the graduate to the carving board with two #10 1¼" flathead wood screws.

The graduate mounted on the carving board. I have painted mine with a light blue wash to help the cuts standout. I suggest that before you make a cut called for in the book that you look ahead to the next couple of pictures. Looking ahead in most cases will help you gain a perception of what you need to accomplish.

Use a V-parting tool to separate the shoe from the gown. I am using a 10mm 90 degree V-tool. Angle the V-tool so you only remove wood from the shoe area. **When using a gouge, remember to keep your free hand on the gouge or behind the path of the gouge. Gouges and even knives sometime have a mind of their own.**

The completed removal of wood. I'm doing a little more rounding on the heel.

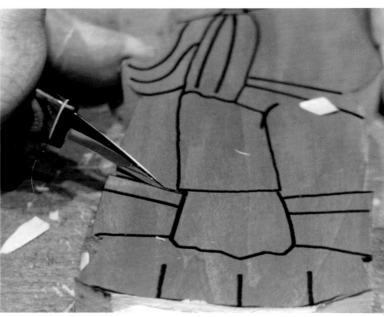

The completed cut.

Cut a stop at the top of the diploma.

Remove wood from the shoe to the depth of approximately ¼" rounding the heel and toe as you cut. I am using a ⅝" No. 2 sweep gouge.

Make several V-tool cuts, one on top of another, from the bottom of the hair to the stop. Angle the V-tool so you don't remove wood from the arm.

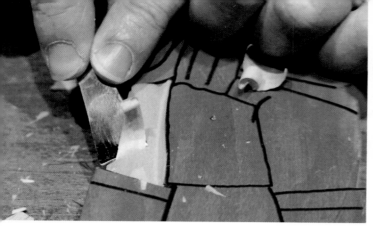

Starting at the bottom of the hair, remove wood back to the diploma. This will drop the gown back and let the arm stand out.

The completed cuts of the last four pictures.

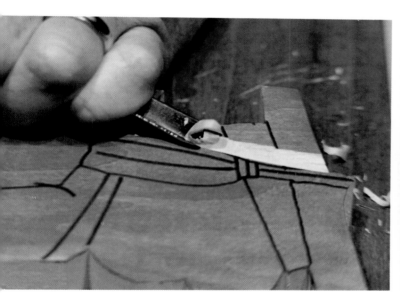

Make several V-tool cuts from the bottom of the tassel to the top of the mortar board.

Redraw the hair line and two hat lines. V-tool the lines.

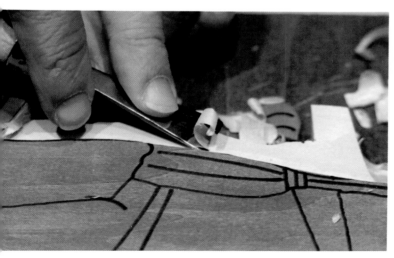

Cut the level of the wood on the gown, hair, and mortar board back approximately ¼".

Use your gouge to taper the hair into the V-tool line of the hat. Taper the gown into the hair line.

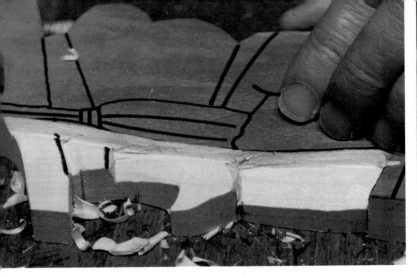

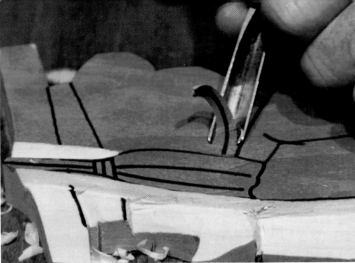

The completed work on the hair and gown. The hair drops back lower than the hat and the gown drops back lower than the hair.

V-tool to the stop cut. This is a deep cut.

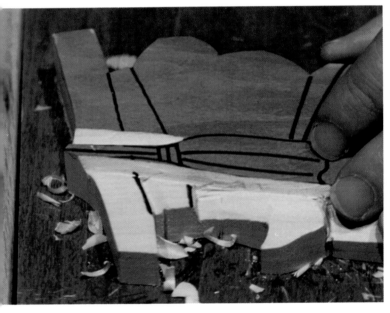

V-tool from the clasp on the tassel to the edge of the mortar board.

V-tool from the bottom of the tassel to the V-cut made in the previous picture. V-tool from the top of the tassel to the V-cut you just completed. This photo shows the completed cuts.

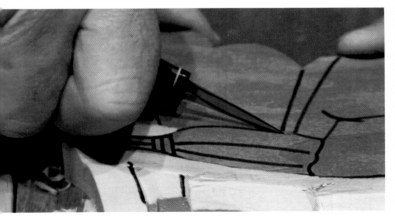

Make a stop cut where the line that defines the head intersects with the tassel.

V-tool the line that defines the bottom of the mortar board. You can see that I have angled my V-tool so that I do not remove any wood from the hat.

Trim the wood away from the hat to the depth you cut it on the back part of the hat.

Shape the face with your gouge rounding it toward the hat, gown, and carving board. I like to taper the face toward the carving board at about a 45 degree angle.

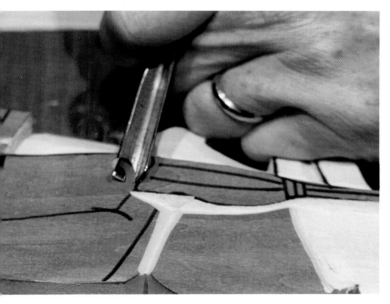

Run your V-tool around the bottom of the tassel.

Draw a line to define where you want the nose to separate from the cheek. Make a stop cut on the line.

Cut a stop on the line that separates the face from the hat.

Use your gouge to cut back to the stop. The angle of the gouge will determine the shape of the cheek.

Cut back to the stop from the other direction with your gouge or knife at about the same angle.

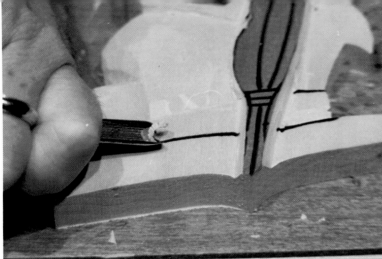

Redraw the edge of the hat. V-tool the line.

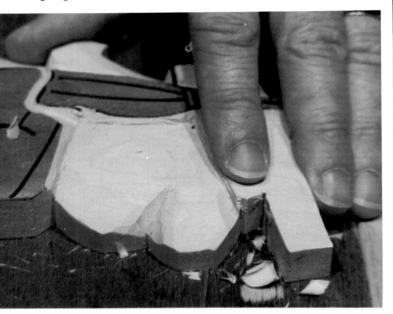

The completed cuts to set the nose.

Shape the shoulder and chest area. You can see how much wood I removed by looking at the remaining blue wood and edge of the carving.

I am using a 10mm No. 7 gouge to create a shallow valley between the nose and face. Make several scooping cuts. Check your work. Make more cuts if needed.

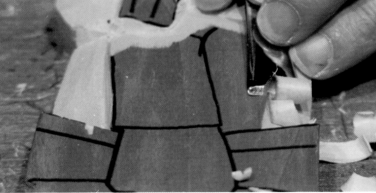

Make a stop cut on the line that defines the top of the diploma. Trim back to the stop with your gouge. The gown needs to drop off toward the board.

V-tool from the shoulder to the stop cut on the diploma. This pictures shows the completed V-cut.

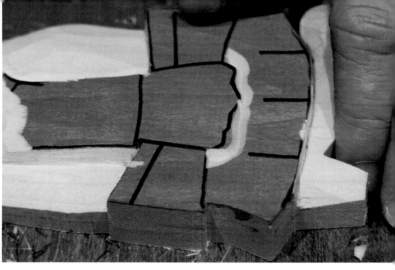

V-tool from the middle of the hand to one side of the diploma. V-tool from the middle of the hand to the other side. This picture shows the completed cuts.

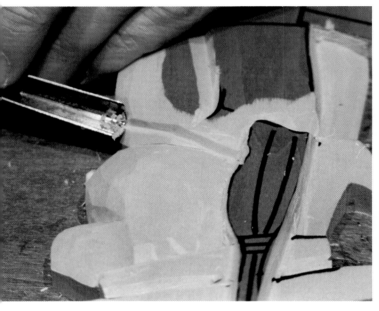

Redraw the collar of the gown. V-tool the line.

Use your gouge to drop back the wood approximately ¼" on the bottom of the gown.

Make stop cuts on the bottom side of the diploma.

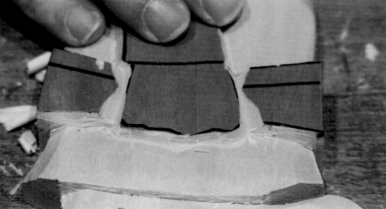

Use a small V-tool to separate the hand from the diploma. As you make the cuts, work to give the hand some definition.

V-tool the line that defines the top of the hand.

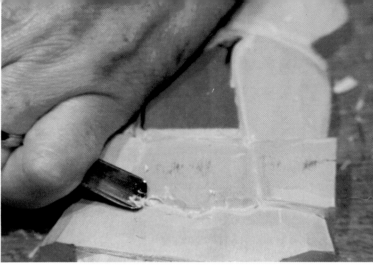

Use your V-tool to define the knuckles of the hand.

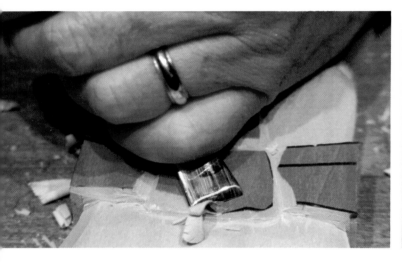

Round the hand and diploma. I have turned over my No. 2 sweep gouge so that the concave part of the gouge is doing the cutting.

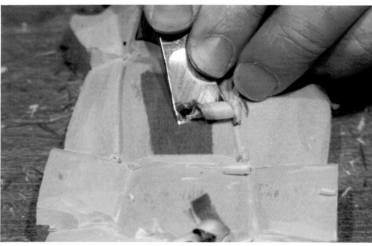

Round the arm. It should drop away toward the body.

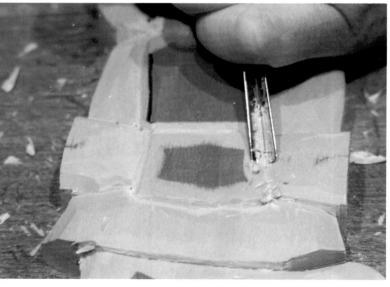

After the hand is rounded, go back and define the edges with some V-tool cuts on each side. Work to really bring out the hand.

Define the edges of the clasp on the tassel with a veiner.

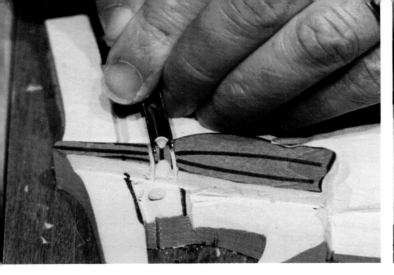

Use a small U-gouge to cut away some wood between the lines. Round the clasp in the process.

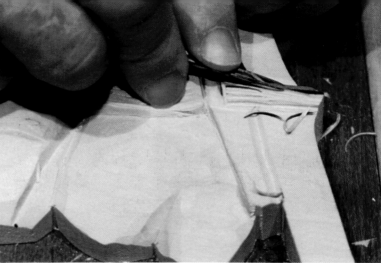

Move to the part of the tassel above the clasp. Use your veiner to add some detail.

I am using a 5mm No. 9 U-gouge to put some shape into the tassel.

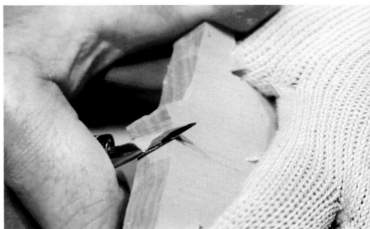

Remove the graduate from the carving board. Use your knife to remove the saw marks from the top of the mortar board. Define the top of the tassel. I've put on a carving glove just in case the knife takes on a mind of its own.

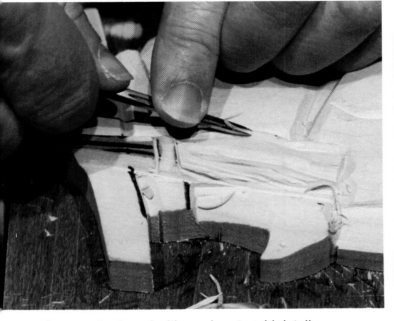

Go over the tassel with a veiner to add detail.

Add detail to the tassel on top of the mortar board with a veiner.

Use your knife to shape the hair to your liking. Add texture to the hair with a V-tool or U-gouge. I'm using a 5mm U-gouge.

Use your knife to shape the shoe to your liking.

Carve away the saw marks from the back and front of the hat, giving them a rounded shape. I'm doing some final shaping on the nose.

Draw the sole line. Outline the foot. Use a small V-tool on the sole line.

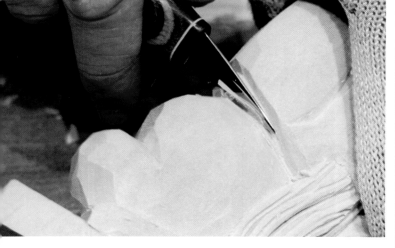

Clean the saw marks from the face, front of the gown, and diploma. All the saw marks should be removed from the carving at this time. I'm giving the collar a concave look.

Use a veiner to separate the foot from the shoe.

Draw the edge of the diploma. Cut a stop. Trim back to the stop.

If you have not already done so, clean the saw marks off the ends of the diploma. Draw the roll of the diploma on each end and use a veiner on the lines.

Use a V-tool to put some wrinkles in the bottom of the gown. I did not extend the cuts to the diploma.

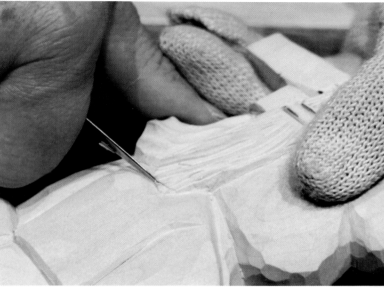

Make a stop cut around the bottom of the tassel. Trim back to it. This photo gives some good perspective to the collar.

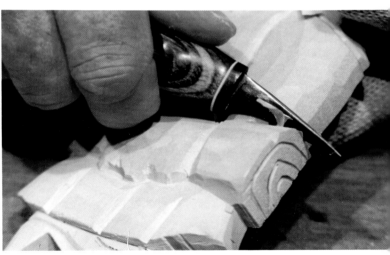

Look over the carving for saw marks, chips, or burrs which need removed. Finish any rounding which still needs to be done.

The completed carving. Because of the thickness of the carving, I believe it is helpful to attach the carving to some kind of base. This is especially important if the shoe has a long toe on it. It can be easily broken. I have used a ¾″ x 1½″ x 4½″ rectangle for the base. You can paint or stain the base. I usually make the base 1 to 1½″ longer than the shoe and then center the carving.

Pattern is shown at 50% of actual size. To restore to actual size enlarge at 200% on a photocopying machine. If you choose to carve the pattern this size I would suggest ⅜″ thick wood. The grain runs head to toe.

Cowboy

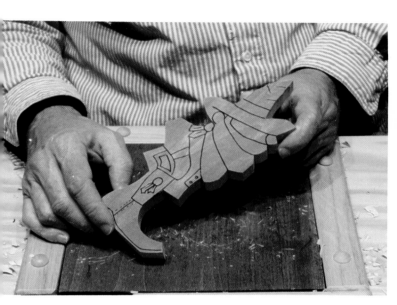

Use carbon paper to transfer the pattern to ¾" thick wood. The grain runs head to toe. Cut out your cowboy using a band saw, coping, or scroll saw. If you choose to use the carving board approach, then attach the cowboy to the carving board with two #10 1¼" flathead wood screws. I have painted the cowboy with a blue wash to help the cuts standout. You don't need to do that to yours.

Since the shirt and boot need to be cut back the deepest, we will begin there. Draw the dotted line at the handle of the gun. Use your knife to cut a stop on the dotted line and around the bottom of the gun handle.

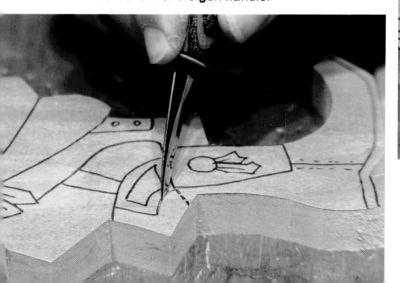

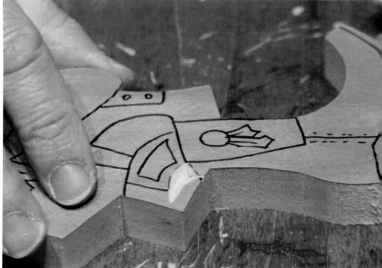

Use a V-parting tool to cut back the stop on the dotted line. This picture shows the completed cut. I'm using an 10mm 90 degree V-tool.

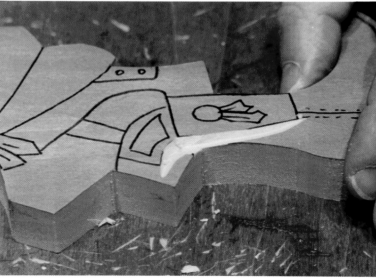

V-tool from the base of the holster to your first V-tool cut. This cut will help the holster stand out from the boot.

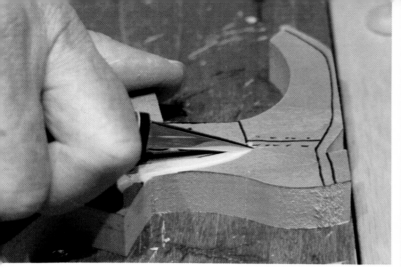

Make a stop just below the bottom of the holster.

Drop the boot back approximately ¼". Do some preliminary rounding of the boot. I am using a ⅝" No. 2 sweep gouge.

V-tool back to the stop. The completed cut.

The completed cuts.

Use your V-tool to drop the shirt below the handle of the gun.

Make a V-tool cut in front of the holster.

Use a small V-tool to define the handle on the gun and the finger tips.

I used my knife, a 6mm No. 7 palm gouge, and a ⅝" No. 2 gouge to remove the wood between the arm and bandanna and in front of the hand. Drop the wood back approximately ¼".

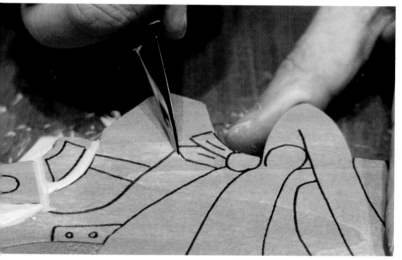

Make a stop cut on the bandanna.

Make stop cuts around the two ends of the bandanna.

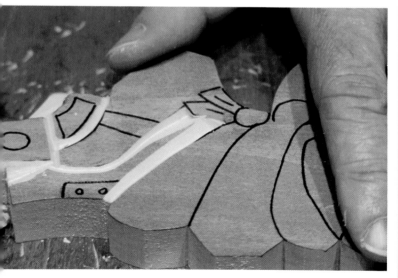

Make two V-tool cuts back to the stop. Angle your V-tool so wood is only removed from the shirt. This picture shows the completed cuts.

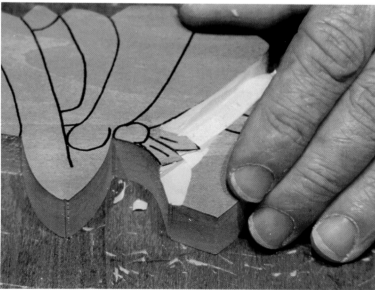

Cut back to the stops dropping the wood around the two ends.

Round off the arm and elbow toward the carving board.

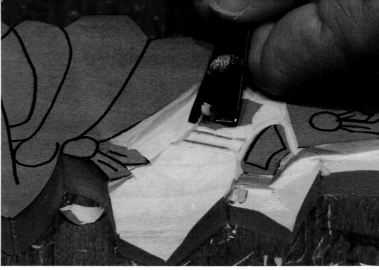

I'm using a No. 2 sweep gouge to round the hand.

Use a small V-tool on the lines which define the cuff.

I like to use an eye-punch to define buttons. They come in various diameters and are available from most wood carving supply catalogs.

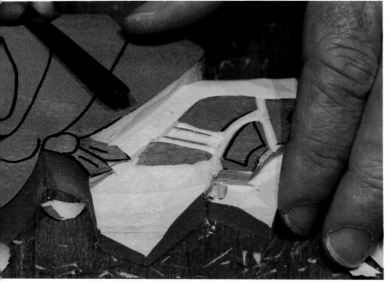

U-gouge between the two V-tool lines on the cuff. This picture shows the completed cuts.

Draw the lines between the fingers. Draw a middle line and then split the distance on each side of that line with another line. Run a veiner along the lines between the fingers to create a separation.

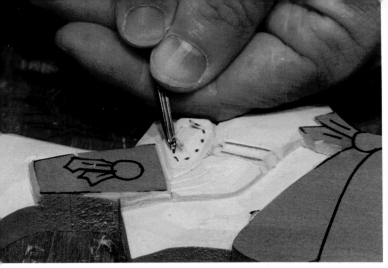

Use a veiner to add some detail to the handle of the gun.

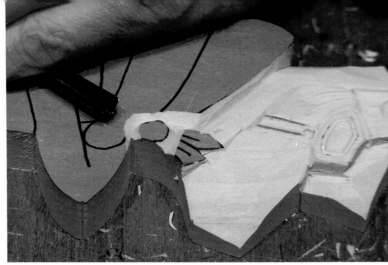

Run your V-tool around the knot on the bandanna.

Use your knife or gouge to "knock" the corners off the holster. I'm knocking off the top edge of the holster.

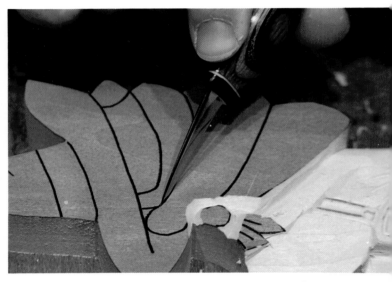

Make a stop cut in front of the ear on the beard line.

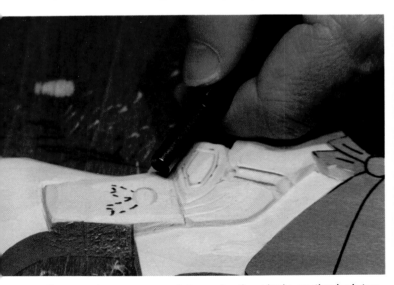

I've used an eye punch to make the circle on the holster. Use a veiner on the lines to define the tassels.

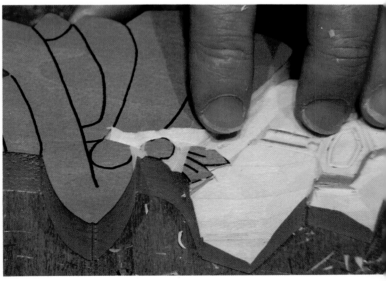

V-tool from the knot to the stop cut. Don't remove any wood from the ear.

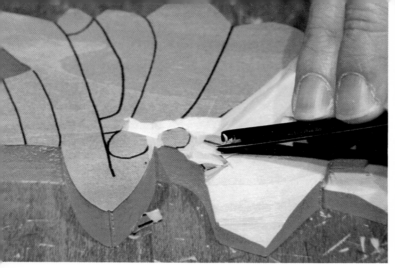

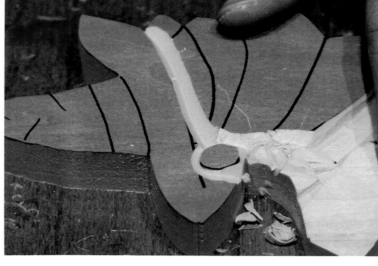

V-tool the hat line stopping the cut at the ear.

Shape the knot to your liking. I took a bandanna and tied it around a chair and then studied the knot and carved it accordingly. This helped me to carve what I saw rather than trying to create what I think a knot might look like.

Taper the back of the hat toward the carving board. Remove wood from behind the ear. A combination of gouge and V-tool cuts works best. You are working to drop the hat below the depth of the knot of the bandanna.

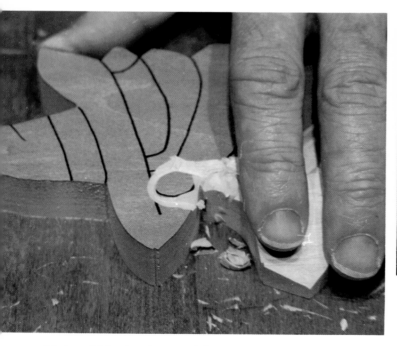

Make a V-tool cut around the ear.

Draw a line from the ear to within a ¼" of the back edge of the hat. V-tool straight to the ear. Turn your V-tool so you only remove wood below the line. You are working to create the illusion that the hat is curving around the back of the head.

26

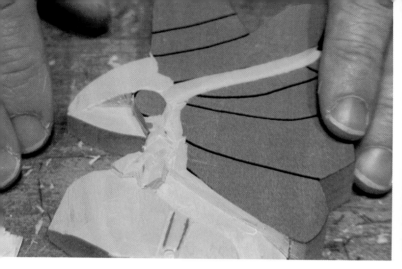

The completed cuts.

Make a V-tool cut on the line which defines the top of the bandanna.

Make a deep V-tool cut on the top hat line. This photo shows the completed cut.

Slope the brim toward the carving board. Use your knife or gouge to "knock" the edges off the top of the hat. Continue to work with your tool, until you have the top of the hat dropped back approximately ¼" from the brim of the hat.

Shape the face with your gouge rounding it toward the hat, bandanna, and carving board. I like to taper the face toward the carving board at about a 45 degree angle.

The completed shaping and rounding of the face.

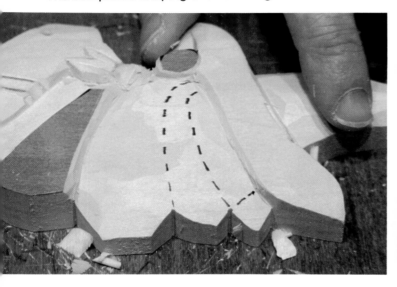

Draw the mustache and a line for the nose.

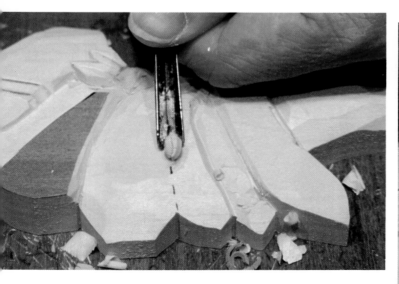

V-tool the mustache lines. V-tool the line for the nose starting the cut at the edge of the face and stopping at the brim of the hat.

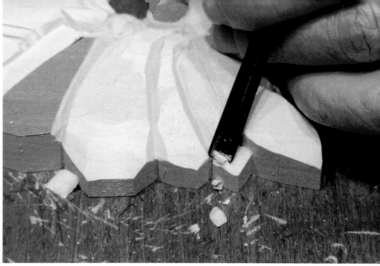

Now make a second V-tool cut on the line for the nose. Start in the middle of the line and cut toward the carving board. This cut will help give the nose a rounded look. Use you knife to do any final rounding on the nose.

Round the bandanna toward the face, shirt, and carving board.

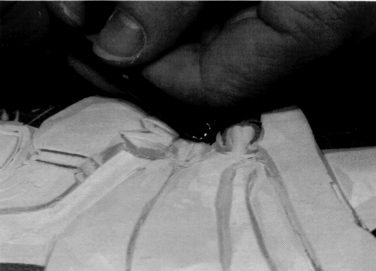

Use a small U-gouge to scoop the wood out of the middle of ear.

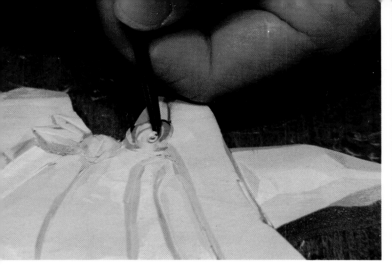

Run a veiner around the inside of the ear to add some definition. Use your knife to round off the ear sloping it into the head.

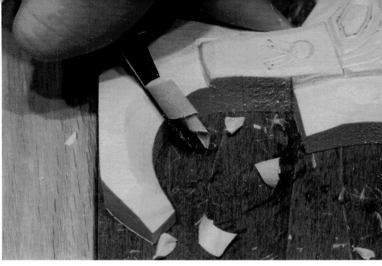

Turn your attention to the boot. Use the knife to complete any shaping which needs to be done.

At the front of the ear push a U-gouge straight in to create the tragus. This is the projection from the face into the middle of the ear. Take a look at someone's ear. It's kind of like a flap.

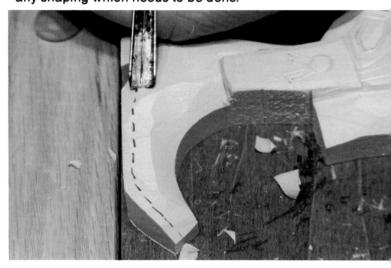

Draw on the sole. Use a small V-tool on the line.

Make several V-tool cuts on the bandanna to add some wrinkles.

Remove the cowboy from the carving board. Round and remove saw marks as you work your way up the back of the boot, shirt, arm, and hat. I have put on a carving glove just in case the knife takes on a mind of its own. Which it has done is the past. I can't explain how and when it does so the carving glove is a good idea.

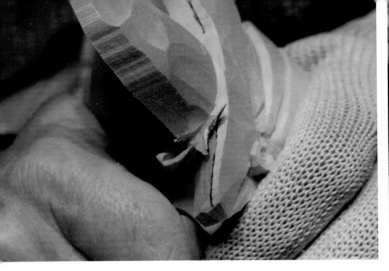

Hollow out the brim of the hat. I have drawn a line to define the brim so I won't cut into the edge of the hat. Round the hat removing all the saw marks.

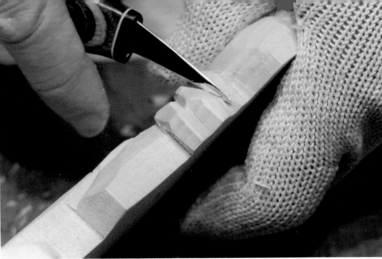

Use your knife to complete the V-tool cuts on the bandanna. Remove any saw marks from the chin, bandanna, and front of the shirt.

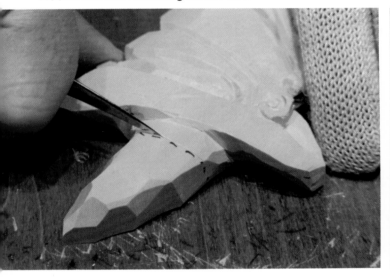

Draw on the hat band; cut a stop on the line. Cut back to the stop.

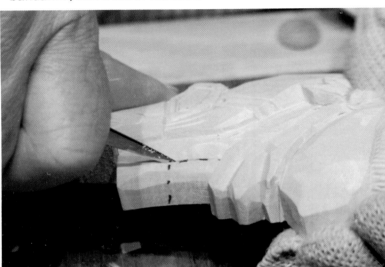

Draw on the shirt flap. Cut a stop on the lines. Cut back to the stop.

Now it's time to finish the mustache. Before you start on the mustache, round the nose to your liking. Use your veiner to add the whiskers on the mustache. **Be sure to place your hand in such a way that if you slip with the tool you won't stab yourself.**

If you have an eye punch, set the buttons. If not, then draw on the buttons. Cut a stop around them; trim back to the stop.

Draw the line to define the front edge of the holster. Make a stop cut on the line. Trim back to the stop.

Add some wrinkles to the boot. This is accomplished by cutting a slice with the knife then cutting back the other way.

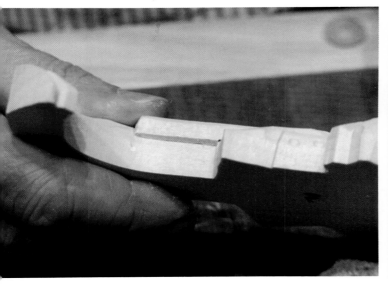

The completed cut. The boot should drop back deeper than the holster.

Make the same V-cuts on the back and front of the boot.

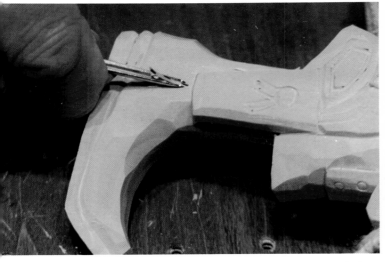

Draw a line from the bottom of the holster to the sole. This is the seam of the boot. Use a veiner on the line.

Use a U-gouge to remove some wood between the wrinkles. The completed U-gouge cuts.

Use a dull pointed nail to add whiskers to the chin. You simply push the nail into the wood enough to make an indention.

Use your knife to put any finishing touches or details on the carving. If you have a pattern wheel, you can add some stitching marks to the boot, gun holster, and flap of the shirt. Also, go over the carving with your knife to "clean" unwanted chips or burrs of wood.

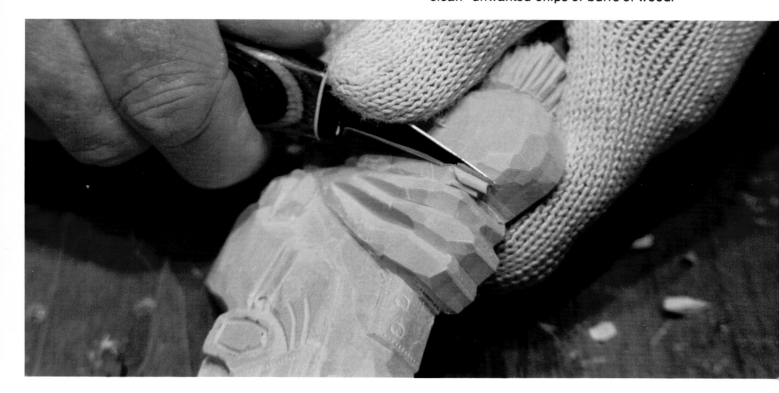

The completed carving. Because of the thickness of the carving, I believe it is helpful to attach the carving to some kind of base. This is especially important if the shoe has a long toe on it. It can be easily broken. I have used a ¾" x 1½" x 4" board for the base. You can paint or stain the base. I usually make the base 1 to 1½" longer than the shoe and then center the carving.

Pattern is shown at 50% of actual size. To restore to actual size enlarge at 200% on a photocopying machine. If you choose to carve the pattern this size I would suggest ⅜" thick wood. The grain runs head to toe.

Basketball Player

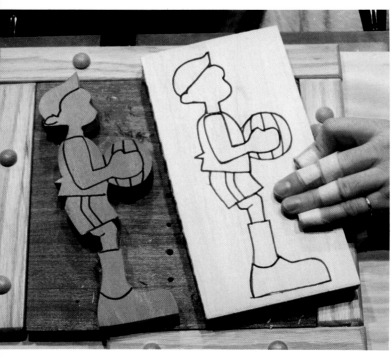

Use carbon paper to transfer the pattern to ¾" thick wood. The grain runs head to toe. Cut out your player using a band saw, coping, or scroll saw. If you choose to use the carving board, attach the basketball player with two #10 1¼" flathead wood screws. I painted the player with a light blue wash to help the cuts standout. You don't need to do that to yours.

Since the leg and shoe need to be cut back the deepest, we will begin there. Use a V-parting tool to separate the leg from the shorts. I prefer to use a 10mm 90 degree V-tool. Angle the V-tool so you only remove wood from the leg area.

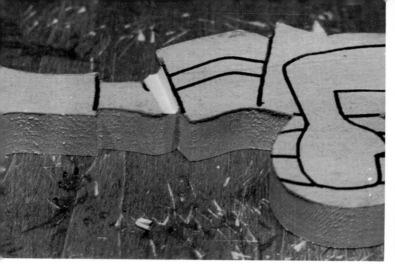

The completed cut.

Draw the shoe and sock line. Define them with the V-tool.

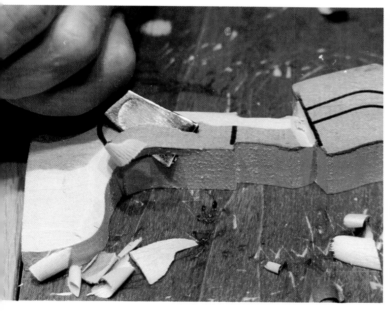

Remove wood to the depth of approximately ¼" from the leg and tennis shoe. Do some preliminary rounding of the tennis shoe, sock, and leg. I am using a ⅝" No. 2 sweep gouge.

V-tool the line separating the jersey from the shorts. Angle the V-tool so you only remove wood from the shorts. This picture shows the cut as well as the completed V-cuts on the shoe and sock.

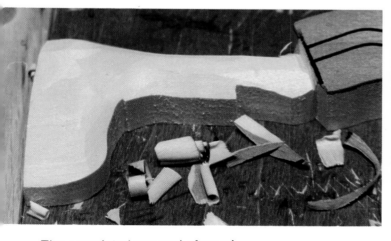

The completed removal of wood.

Draw a line down the center of the shorts. Round them on each side of the line. The shorts need to "drop away" from the line.

Use a knife to make stop cuts at the top and bottom of the neck. Trim back to the stops to remove wood from the neck. Drop the neck back approximately ¼".

Starting at the elbow, make several V-tool cuts on the line which defines the back of the arm. Don't remove any wood from the arm. You are working to drop back the wood behind the arm. These cuts will allow the arm to stand out.

The completed V-tool cuts.

Round the back of the jersey.

Make several V-tool cuts from the wrist to the elbow.

Use a gouge to cut back to the arm removing wood from the jersey. The jersey needs to drop off toward the carving board.

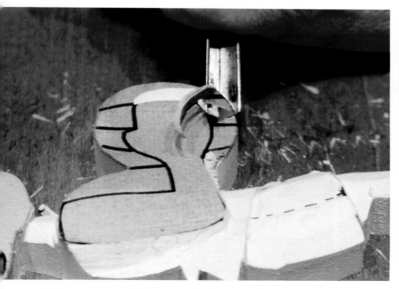

V-tool around the hand sloping the ball toward the carving board.

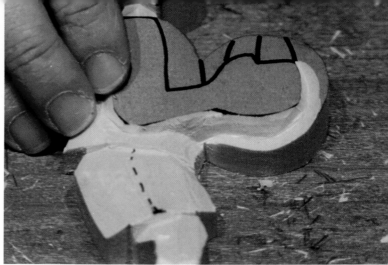

The completed V-tool cuts around the arm and hand. The wood from the jersey and ball have been cut back the same depth.

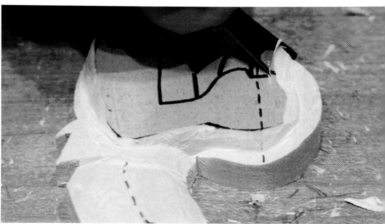

Draw a line down the center of the hand and ball. Round the wood toward the carving board.

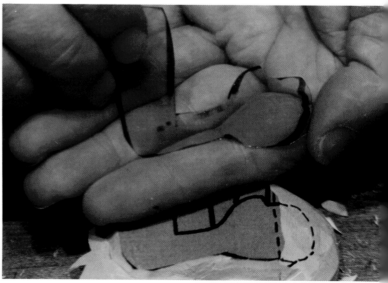

Redraw the hand. So I get everything right, I made a clear plastic template which I can lay on the carving and trace around.

 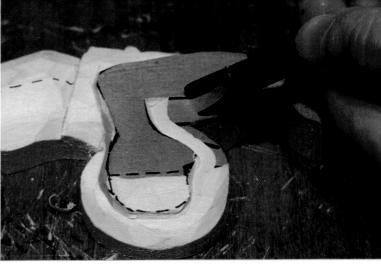

V-tool around the hand stopping at the inside of the elbow. Don't remove wood from the hand. This picture shows the completed cut.

V-tool along the arm stopping at the elbow. Angle the V-tool so you don't remove any wood from the arm.

The completed V-tool cut along the arm.

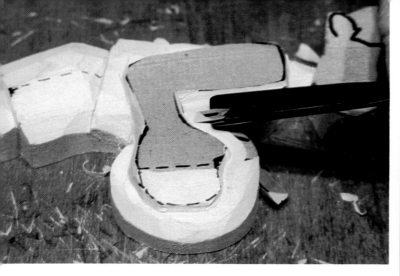

Make a V-tool cut between the stomach and basketball stopping at the arm. This cut will help you later in shaping the ball and stomach.

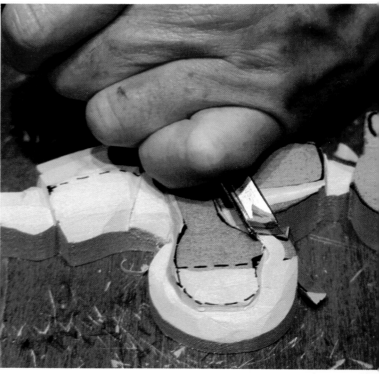

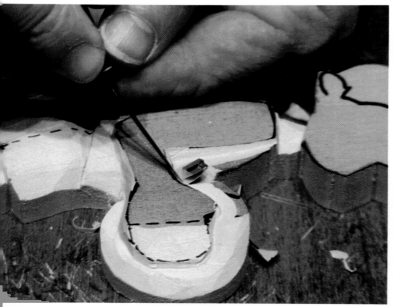

Pop out the wood left from the V-tool cut.

Round the top of the ball. This is a combination of V-tool and gouge cuts around the hand. You are working to drop the wood on the ball lower than the hand.

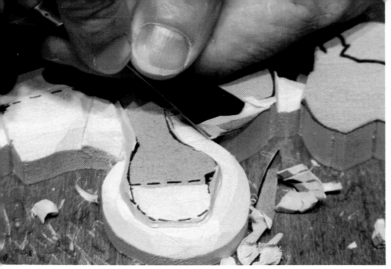

Round off the chest and stomach.

Use a gouge or knife to round and shape the hand.

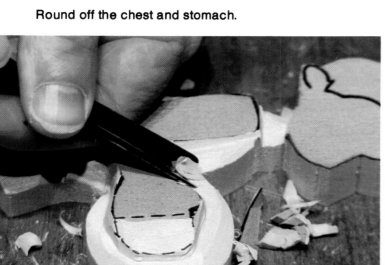

After some rounding of the chest and stomach, I find it helpful to make another V-tool cut to separate the stomach and ball. This cut is away from the arm.

Draw a line to define the front of the thumb.

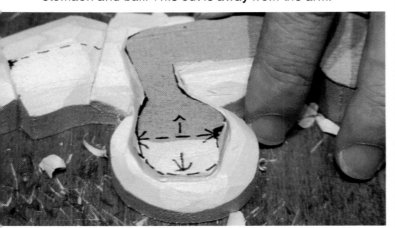

Round the hand. It needs to be rounded in 4 directions. If you put your hand on a basketball, it conforms to the rounding of the ball. The hand should not be left flat. You might have to remove more wood from the basketball to gain the desired effect.

Make a V-cut on the line.

Make a stop cut in front of the thumb.

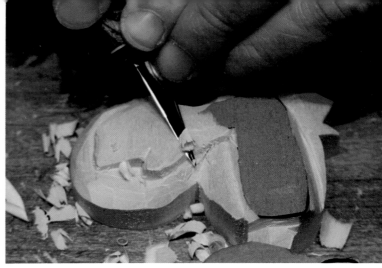

Look over the hand. Does anymore shaping need to be done? I am working to make the wrist smaller and more round.

Define the edge of the first finger by cutting a stop. Pop out the triangle created by the stop cuts.

Use your V-tool or knife to round and set the length of the fingers.

The completed defining of the thumb.

Draw the lines between the fingers. Draw a middle line and then split the distance on each side of that line with another line. Run a small veiner along the lines between the fingers to create a separation.

Run a small V-tool over the veiner lines to create more separation between the fingers. The next picture shows the completed veiner and V-tool cuts.

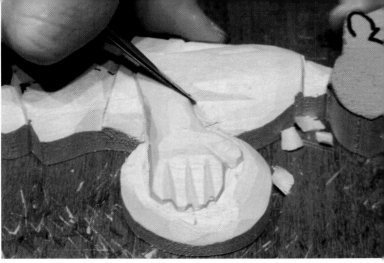

Continue to round the arm shaping it into the wrist. Make a V-cut on the inside of the elbow to add a wrinkle.

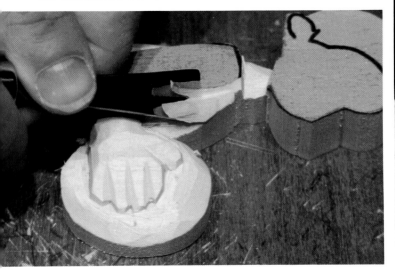

Shape the front and back of the shoulder. I have turned my gouge over allowing the concave surface of the gouge to cut the wood. This produces a rounded cut.

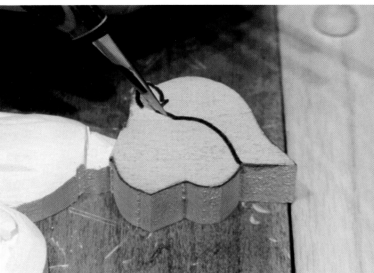

Make a stop cut on the hair line above the front of the ear.

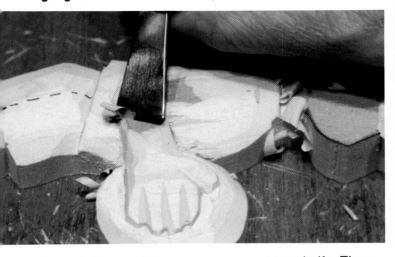

Round the arm. You can use a gouge or knife. There should be no flat spots left on the arm.

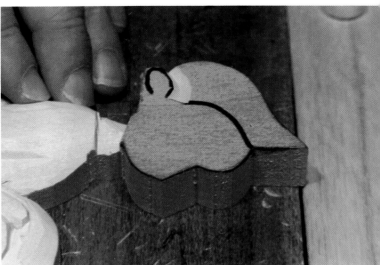

V-tool back to the stop cut. Angle the V-tool so you don't remove wood from the ear.

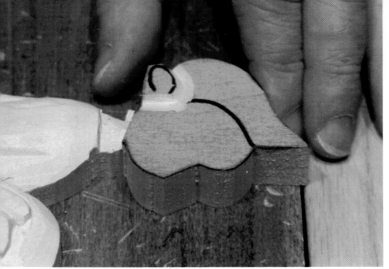

Make a V-tool cut in front of the ear.

Use the V-tool to separate the face from the hair.

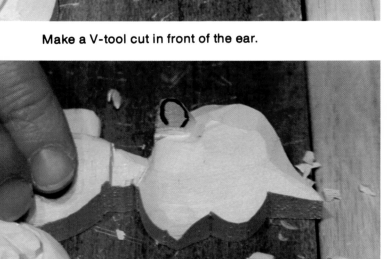

Round the head removing wood toward the front and back leaving the ear alone.

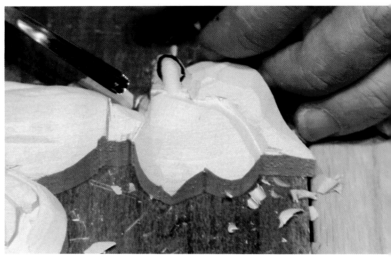

Shape the inside of the ear with a U-gouge.

Redraw the hair line.

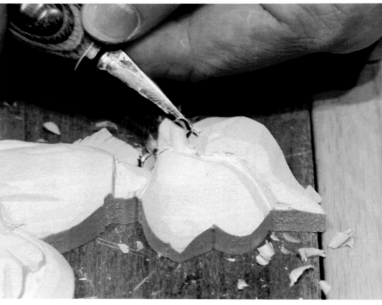

The knife works well for the final shaping of the ear. The ear needs to flow into the face.

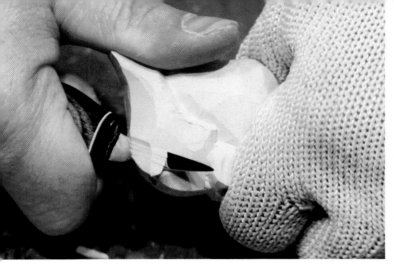

Remove the player from the carving board. Use your knife to shape the hair in the style you wish. I have put on a carving glove just in case the knife takes on a mind of its own. Which it has done in the past. I can't explain how and when it does so the carving glove is a good idea.

I am using a 6mm No. 7 sweep palm gouge to remove wood from behind the ear. **When using a V-tool or gouge without the carving board, be sure to place your hand in such a way that if you slip with the tool you won't stab yourself.**

Draw a dotted line where you want the nose to be separated from the cheek. Cut a slice on each side of the line with my knife. These two cuts create a V-cut.

I am using a 10mm No. 7 gouge to make several scooping cuts to separate the nose from the cheek. Make a cut. Check your work. You are trying to create a shallow valley between the cheek and nose.

Round the nose, chin and neck.

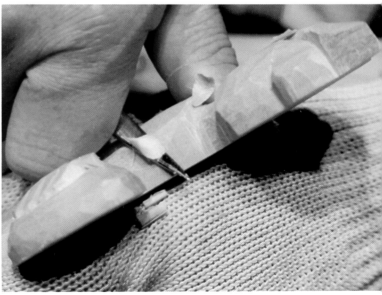

Continue to work your way down the front of the player removing saw marks. Rounding the carving as you go.

Round the basketball removing all the saw marks.

Round the leg and sock.

Remove the saw marks from the back of the jersey. Make V-cuts to define the wrinkles on the back of the jersey.

Shape the shoe to your liking. Draw the sole line; use a veiner on the line.

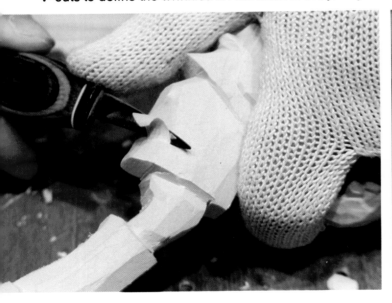

Remove the saw marks from the front and back of the shorts.

Draw on some detail lines. Make a stop cut on the top of the shoe.

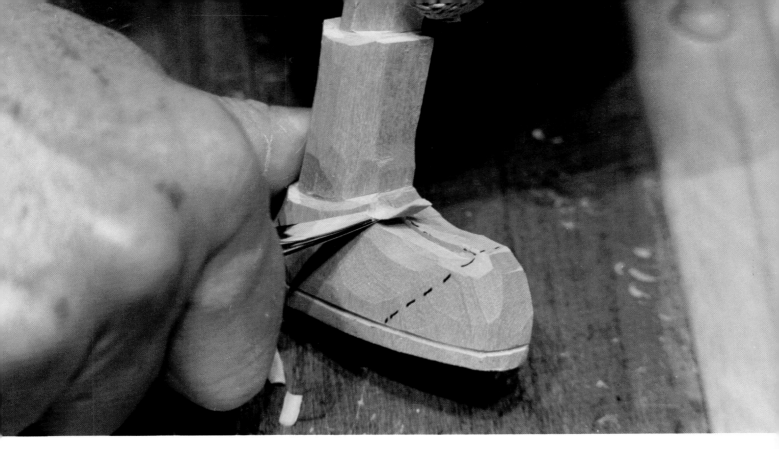

Cut back to the stop lowering the wood just enough to give the area where the laces lay a raised effect.

Use a veiner to define the detail lines. This picture also shows the completed stop and wood removal for the area where the laces are.

Draw on the shoe laces. Use a veiner to define them.

Use a pattern wheel to add stitching marks to the shoe.

48

I am using a U-gouge to add some indentions in the sole.

Use a U-gouge to add wrinkles to the sock. **Remember to think about a safe hand placement.** The deeper the cuts the deeper the wrinkles.

The completed sock and shoe.

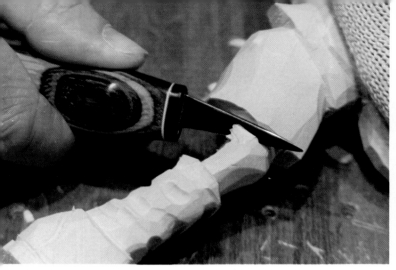

Do any rounding which still needs to be done on the leg. Use you knife to add wrinkles to the back of the knee.

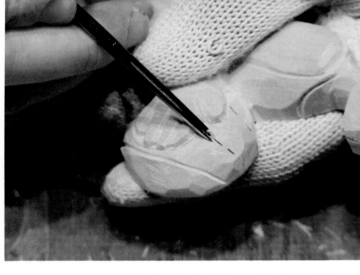

Draw the seams on the basketball. Start with the middle line and then angle the other two lines slightly toward it. This should give the ball more of a rounded look.

Add texture to the hair with a V-tool or U-gouge. I'm using a U-gouge.

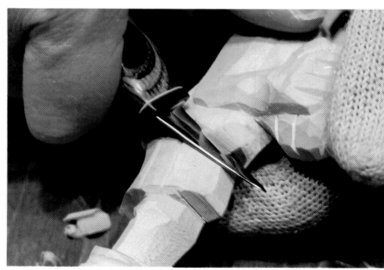

Depending upon the jersey style you want for your carving, draw the detail lines on the jersey and shorts. Use a veiner to define them. Of course, if you're doing this carving for a friend or child then look at their uniform. I have a friend who collects basketball cards so I look at them for detailing the uniform.

Use your knife to put any finishing touches or details on the carving. Also, you should go the carving with your knife to "clean" unwanted chips or burrs of wood.

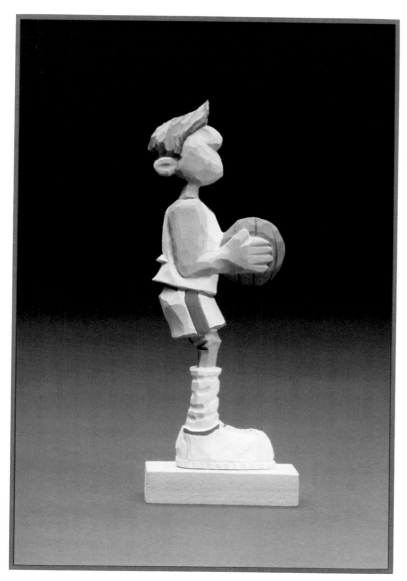

Because of the thickness of the carving, I believe it is helpful to attach the carving to some kind of base. This is especially important if the shoe has a long toe on it. It can be easily broken. I have used a ¾" x 1½" x 3¼" board for the base, you can paint or stain the base. I usually make the base 1 to 1½" longer than the shoe and then center the carving.

Pattern is shown at 50% of actual size. To restore to actual size enlarge at 200% on a photocopying machine. If you choose to carve the pattern this size I would suggest ⅜" thick wood. The grain runs head to toe.

Gallery and Patterns

All of the patterns can be carved from ¾" thick wood. I prefer basswood for these projects. On some projects, you might want to use 1" stock. The additional depth will give you freedom for more detail. If you reduce the pattern, you might want to choose ½" stock. You can use 1¾" wood and make some larger carvings. Don't be afraid to experiment with pattern enlargements or reductions.

Mike loves to draw dragons and kept asking me about putting a "dragon pattern" in the book. To keep him content and happy, I included a "Dragon."

The patterns are shown at 50% of actual size. To restore to actual size enlarge at 200% on a photocopying machine. If you choose to carve the pattern this size I would suggest ⅜" thick wood. The grain runs head to toe.

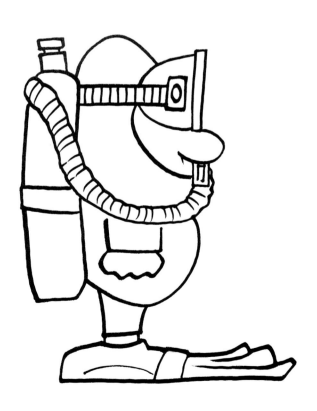

56

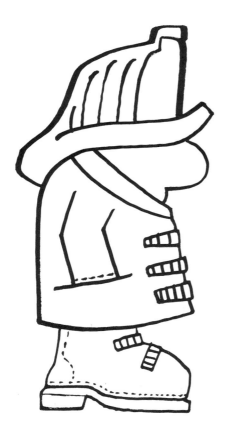

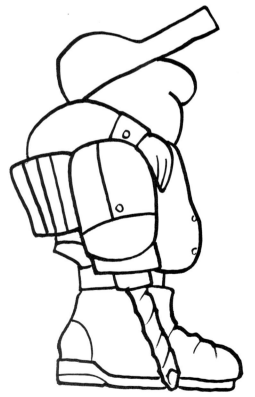